ONE YEAR THERE

One Soldier's Year In South Korea During 1968

Robert Denis Holewinski

Copyright © 2014 Robert Holewinski

All rights reserved.
No parts of this publication may
be reproduced or transmitted
in any form or by any means, electronic
or mechanical, including photocopy,
recording, or any information storage
and retrieval system, without permission
in writing from the author.

I have tried to recreate events,
locales and conversations
from my memories of them.
In order to maintain their
anonymity in some instances
I have changed the names
of individuals and places,
I may have changed some
identifying characteristics and
details such as physical
properties, occupations
and places of residence.

for Deb
who endured
all my starts and stops
and encouraged me
to write this book

An Introduction

The following poems are memories of the year 1968 in South Korea. They are memories of the soldiers assigned to my unit, located in a small outpost, hidden in the mountains of that country. These poems are snapshots of life on that nuclear missile base which was high on the North Korean list of targets. Indeed, we were always on the alert for possible infiltrators who had come into South Korea and who were expected to be heading toward our camp.

Although these poems can be looked at as a military war story, there are no battles or heroes or military campaigns. Rather, these poems will show life in a small army base in Korea during a very anxious and confusing time, always with the constant possibility of a full scale war.

That year was filled with news items about the two Koreas with the capture of the USS Pueblo by the North Koreans, her crew paraded through the news media, accused of being spies, then the killing of Robert Kennedy, and the killing of Martin Luther King. Also during that period, a team of 12 North Korean assassins got to within a few blocks of the South Korean presidential palace before being stopped.

It was my intention in writing these poems that the reader could come away with a better understanding of what life was like in 1968 at an army base in South Korea. It was also my intention in writing these poems that I would purge the phantoms that have been dwelling inside me since living "One Year There".

The years 1966 through 1969 have been called the 'Second Korean War' by military historians.

chapter 1 – the classroom

from the back of the classroom
attention is called
loudly demanding
to be obeyed
the soldier students spring to their feet
in unison wood chair legs scrape
decades old dull worn wood floors

hard heeled shoes clack in unison
as the two officers march forward
one is marine and one is army
the marine lieutenant foss
bounds up onto the low stage
a serious career lieutenant without humor
foss is a field commissioned officer
given his gold bar while in vietnam
silent he now stands
silent at the podium silent
he shuffles papers looks up
to scan the soldier's faces before him
looking briefly into their eyes

all too young he thinks

gentlemen take your seats
there is more scraping of chair legs
gentlemen your orders have been issued
i have seen your orders
all of you (all of you) are being assigned
for duty in vietnam
most of you will not be coming back alive
(will not be coming back alive)
artillery surveyors are not needed in vietnam
it is jungle warfare without known targets
no bases or fronts or safe zones
instead you will be forward observers
with a compass map walkie-talkie rifle
you will search the jungle for the vietcong
most of you will not be coming back alive
once you find the vietcong
you will call in their coordinates
for immediate bombing and shelling

those first explosions will tell the vietcong
that you are there you are near
they have been found by you

you are the reason for the bombs

(will not be coming back alive)

gentlemen from that first explosion

they will do whatever is necessary

to find you capture you kill you

they know the jungle well

i am telling you so you can prepare

yourself for what lies ahead

to prepare both here and at home

graduation will be in two weeks

processing begins after graduation

for your transfer to vietnam

gentlemen it has been a privilege

wish i had better news for you

wish you all the best of luck

      that is all

      that is all

      gentlemen class dismissed

there is again scrapping of chair legs

on the floor as we stand

two officers move through the building

without pause without any more words

(will not be coming back alive)

the normally noisy raucous bus ride

back to the barracks

       is traveled in silence

       thoughts being elsewhere

       anywhere but here or now

chapter 2 – the printed headline

while waiting
in the morning mess line
i read the printed headline
north korea captures navy ship pueblo
      accusing the crew of spying

her crew then paraded before cameras
marched to a north korean prison
dressed in drab prisoner of war pajamas
      the ship docked as proof of spying

i did not know then that the headlines
would alter the army orders for me
and my past two weeks of trauma
      would end my dying in vietnam

the pueblo's capture changed my orders
with the taking of the navy spy ship
new orders would send me to korea
      where war was expected to reignite

with new orders i would fly to korea

still hearing the prophecy of foss

only now seeing my death

on a snow covered mountain

    rather than in a steamy jungle

while waiting

in the morning mess line

i read the printed headline

chapter 3 – in my hands

in my hands

i had held my orders to vietnam

and i had existed for two weeks

wrapped in a printed paper coffin

orders predicting my short

extremely expendable future

i heard the marine lieutenant repeating

    you will not be coming back alive

believing that i was handed

an all but finalized death sentence

became a prophesied future

that i was unable to escape

living with that pale shadow

saying this was becoming real

    and happening to me

that american ship pueblo

captured off the coast by north korea

her sailor crew called spies

locked away as prisoners of war

and my paper death sentence

        is changed abruptly to korea

where a frantic full scale

military build-up has begun

full war preparations started

accusations and threats in anger spoken

heard on evening news broadcasts

        and covering newspaper front pages

the border of the two countries

overflows with military force and display

it promises a year of extreme

tension and ever present war

this year of the pueblo and colbern

        and one year in korea

        one year there

chapter 4 – fourteen hours

fourteen hours
is the flight time
from seattle to japan to south korea
fourteen hours flying
being tightly cramped
in a boeing 707 tube
packed full with military personnel
with our civilian flight crew
we are part of the military build-up
in preparation for the expected war
near the back of the plane i sit
crammed into the dreadfully tight middle seat
captive between two career sergeants
both are hungry for duty in korea

a possibility of war is nothing to them
in fact they each relish the prospect of war
since war creates chaos
and chaos brings a certain freedom for profit
both sergeants had been to korea before
they talk long about prostitutes and night clubs

a flight attendant hands out cans of soda

and pre-made plastic wrapped sandwiches

we approach japan with the cabin smelling

of a high school gym locker room

we land in japan to refuel

switching to a military flight crew

we are allowed to deplane briefly

a brood of american soldiers cluster

still wearing their jungle fatigues

still wearing mud stained boots

still carrying their weapons

we know they are from vietnam

plucked from some jungle or rice paddy

flown here to a music filled airport terminal

one soldier sits alone

leaning forward rocking

staring down at the floor

holding his M-16 with both hands

he rocks slowly

in the plastic molded seat

continues looking down at the floor tiles

we re-board our plane

the short flight to kimpo airbase

from one island nation

to one peninsula nation

from the modern

to the almost medieval

we land and step from the plane

onto a metal exit staircase

my face gets slapped hard

by the bitterly cold wind

blowing across a barren frozen brown landscape

it is january and winter dances with abandon

snow powdering the countryside

and the distant barren mountaintops

it is a strange and alien landscape i see

with the few scattered buildings

old drab colored military hangers

the korean sky is a clear ice crystal blue

the land is white and brown dirt and dust

duffel bags are flung from the plane

we are told to find our bag

to move quickly to one airplane hanger

      keep moving ladies

   let's go hurry up
   find your duffel bag
   move to that hanger
   walk with a purpose soldier
   walk with a purpose

my jacket and overcoat are worthless barriers
against the sharp clawed korean wind
the airbase personnel wear thick insulated
jackets with fur lined hoods double layer gloves
still looking frozen they watch us
the hanger offers little warmth
where i see my breath exhaled
in small puffed clouds
a line of shivering overcoats slowly move
toward white medical partitions
where medics give air-gun injections
we remove our coats and our shirts
to expose both upper arms
   do not move during the injection
   if you do move
   or tighten your muscle
   during the injection process
   the air pressure will shred your muscle

one step forward to the medic

on my left and the medic on my right

both injections coming at the same time

feeling the burn of the liquid

as it is forced through my skin

and into the arm muscle

a third medic stands ready to give

another injection into my right arm

thin red lines run

from the three injection sites

at the next medical screen

a medic waits holding a large syringe

    drop your pants soldier

    and bend over

he jabs the needle deep

there is more intense burning

after the injection i stand

    not so fast boy

    these are gamma globulin shots

    and you get two

there is a second deep jab

in the other buttock

and more intense burning

    okay soldier

       see you in six months
turning away he shouts next

a brown military bus waits outside
with seats having little padding
 and the vinyl feeling ice cold
the brown landscape passes outside my window
frozen rice paddies and ponds of ice
the bus fills with a fine powdery dust
swirling and drifting sparkling in the sunlight
the continual squeaking and rattling
of the bus becomes louder
as i see korea through streaked windows
a korean man stands near the road
urinates into a roadside ditch
a small trail of steam
rising from his urine stream
houses are small shelters
set among frozen rice paddies
built of whatever material was available
stone boulders making a part of the house
with another part of cement blocks
some have walls of gray tile
while another wall is weathered gray wood

most houses are covered with straw thatch

and look very much like an elephant's back

slanted chimney tubes exit the house

each tube exhaling a thin string

of gray smoke that disappears in the wind

one house appears to have exterior walls

made of old movie posters

it is late afternoon

as my bus arrives

at the army base known as incheon

where i will receive my assignment

tomorrow having to yet experience

my first night in korea

chapter 5 – first night

my first night here
in a corrugated metal quonset hut
crowded with nameless soldiers
both those arriving called turtles
and those leaving called short-timers
the hut contains a tangible darkness
that ignores the single row
of caged light bulbs hanging
from a limp wire attached to the ceiling
casting thick ominous shadows
dancing within the smoke hazed building
bunk beds stick out from the walls
reminding me of grainy sepia photographs
seen of concentration camp barracks
smokey shadows and voices mix
in the air like soaring vultures
the guys who arrived today
are young visibly scared and confused
like me trying to hide our confusion and fear
from the soldiers cycling back stateside
confidently arrogant in appearance

they have survived their year

and in leaving are almost giddy

in well worn fatigues

dried mud spattered boots

most holding a cigarette loosely

between weather cracked fingers

or hanging from cold chapped lips

they sit on the top bunks

telling their stories

with the new guys clustered

around wearing clean uniforms

with still spit polished shoes

in closed mouth silence we listen

as the veterans speak in hushed voices

about the place but a few miles away

    my unit lost two guys just last week

one veteran says calmly

his eyes fixed on his cigarette

    you will hear gun fire day and night

    the gooks plant trip flares and grenades

    buddy of mine got his leg blown clean off

    got my stripes up there

    got shot at far too often

    you do not want to be an easy hit

i make my way to an empty bunk

dropping my duffel bag on the floor

there is talk about escalation and fighting

talk about the assassination team

all killed near the korean president

talk of the navy ship pueblo

her crew locked in a north korean prison

    you see shadows moving

    you know someone is out there

    in the night out there

    probing your defense perimeter

    your tin can alarm clatters in the night

one veteran puffs his cigarette

his audience silent mouths closed tight

    you will hear a rifle crack

    see a brief flash bright

    answered with an automatic burst

    a grenade explodes not so far away

    you hear the shrapnel rain down

    gooks vanish in the dark like ghosts

    we moved once into a good position

    thinking we were unseen invisible quiet

    when we hear gook loudspeakers say

    american soldier in south korea

       you miss home and miss girlfriend
       it was a damned gook talking to our patrol
       she then read our names
       wished one guy a happy birthday
       it can freak you out

one veteran reclines on his bunk
staring at the bunk mattress above
i climb onto a top bunk and sit on the edge
feeling a complete disconnect
feeling my heart beating faster
feeling my fingers tingle from fear
hearing an ocean roaring inside my head
feeling the distortion of reality
a voice now speaks
with the scratchiness of an old vinyl record
playing on a long unused victrola

       you are here for one reason
       to raise holy hell and kick butt
       when the red army comes across
       we had so many firefights
       with the little bastards
       firing rounds exchanging machine gun blasts
       setting off explosions throwing grenades
       stuff that you will not find on evening news

>   day patrols night patrols
>
>   night ambushes bridge duty
>
>   freezing cold icy rain
>
>   fog gloom land mines snipers

his friend adds carefully chosen words

>   listen closely you turtles
>
>   it gets really really cold
>
>   icy with everything frozen
>
>   out on patrol or stuck in a bunker
>
>   then it becomes unbelievably muggy
>
>   unbearably hot never comfortable sweating
>
>   you suck in mosquitoes with every breath
>
>   rats running over your legs at night
>
>   you will see moths the size of birds
>
>   and deer that bark in the morning darkness
>
>   frost and bugs will chew your flesh
>
>   the winter wind will claw at your face
>
>   it will be your own little piece of hell
>
>   but you will tolerate it and get out okay
>
>   keep your eyes and ears open
>
>   keep your head down

the scratchy vinyl record voice speaks

>   this is a real war with real bullets
>
>   with an enemy who wants only to kill you

        real grenades blasting apart the night hours
        floating flares and high explosive rounds
        this is a full throttle hot war
        remember that up there in the zone
feelings of a film noir movie
without a script or writer or director
where we are new extras without names
without any idea of what our role will be
or who would survive the inevitable cut
the lights are extinguished
the talk seems to go underground
with nervous muted words dusting the hut
and drifting clouds of cigarette smoke
and the flaring orange glow of cigarette tips
        a huey helicopter thump-thumps by overhead
        that closeness brings a light snowfall
        of dust drifting down
the coming morning is hours away
and i will sleep little this night

chapter 6 – ward wake up

ward wake up
ward wake up you drunk
wake up and go quick to river
fill sandbags help hold back water
monsoon river wants this village
ward get up now and go

he rolled slowly out of her bed
his military hair matted to his head
his eyes are booze red and puffy
pot belly draping over his army boxers
his breath heavy with whiskey and stale beer

ward stands rubbing his belly burping twice
his fatigues lay mounded on the floor
he hears the clatter of plates in the next room
maybe his village girl is fixing a meal
but mostly he is confused
his mind still asleep
why is he standing beside the bed
something about the river

something about sandbags

his arm feels sore and he rubs it slowly

fighting to collect a solid thought

ward grabs his pants as the room moves

he lifts one leg and almost falls gives up

he sits on the bed pausing to listen

to the rain pounding hard above

still raining he mutters

bending over

to reach one boot passing gas

did you wake me

why did you wake me

a plump korean girl fills the doorway

staring down at ward with mild disgust

her hair pinned up she dries her hands

yes i wake you

i punch you in arm many times

she picks up his other boot handing it to him

you need to get up go help soldiers at river

help them build wall to stop river

you drunk ward i help you with boot laces

get away i can tie my own boots

ward ties a tight sloppy knot

get me my shirt and hat
and do not tell me what to do

ward stumbles to the door
pausing to get his balance
looking at his wedding band
saying to the prostitute i will be back later
she does not reply
only breaks a slight smile
the sergeant is just a customer
one in a history filled with soldiers
but she will be his until his money ends
ward opens the door feels the rain
that has been falling for weeks
and walks toward the river
slipping
he falls flat on his back
lifts himself not caring who saw him
but walks with more caution to the river
where he sees a brown churning monster
steadily growing wider
reaching for the village
already over the road to their new bridge
and flooding into the surrounding rice paddies

soldiers are furiously filling sandbags
building a wall to stop the river's advance
 a desperate barrier
to stop the river

ward watches their assembly line
filling and sealing the bags
passing them along soldier by soldier
he mumbles need a damned cup of coffee
screw the river and the wall i need coffee

ward turns to walk up the hill to the mess hall
the sandbag wall is doing fine without him
but then he spots something in the river
a boat or door or piece of furniture something
what the heck is that he says to himself
drawing his hand
over his chin stubble
he stumbles back to the river's edge
his knees bumping against the sandbag wall
the floating thing is already much closer
rain is washing into his bloodshot eyes
he leans out over the wall

hell i can reach it
ward leans out grabbing the window frame
gripping it and it seeming to grip him as well
jerking him over the wall into the river
as the worthless frame becomes a raft

he is too startled to yell for help
he watches helpless as the sandbag wall
and poncho wearing men whisk away from him
he hears shouts and can see men running
trying to stay with the window frame

the tailor shop butcher shop three bars all flash past
the current pulls ward away from shore
and out into the river channel
becoming a runaway roller coaster
of brown muddy water

like a bug trapped on a leaf
clinging and clawing at the leaf
he feels suddenly sober
being forced to swallow river water
(ward wake up and go quick to river)
he sees soldiers pointing downstream

he fights hard to turn around in the water
only to see a tightly packed spider web
of branches trees roots sticks cloth paper fences
straining the river flood water
rushing under the bridge
he tries a few kicks to move toward shore

he knows his course is unchangeable
he is now too far out in the river
moving too fast toward the bridge
he tightens his grip on the worthless piece of junk
he whispers this is a kick in the ass
with crushing force he is slammed into the debris
the glass shards in the window slice deep
ward feels nothing caught underwater
holding his breath until he no longer can
he then inhales water that is almost injected
into him by the force of the river

his last thoughts
are of his childhood home
going with his older brother
to the water hole to swim
come on jimmy wake up let's go swimming

after the monsoon ends the flood recedes

sending search parties to find ward's body

searching downstream along the river's length

until it joins with the larger han river

the search parties do not find his body

his belongings are boxed

and sent home by the military

to his widow and children

chapter 7 – raining hard

raining hard this day
sergeant archer squeezes through the door
to enter the battery office
archer forms a solid block
a human cube with arms and legs
he recently transferred to colbern
arriving with the monsoon rains
with six years in the military
six years claiming two tours in vietnam

his souvenirs
from there include
a battered album of polaroid photos
snapshots of american soldiers playing soccer
with a vietcong soldier's head
the head being kicked past goal posts
and the soldiers cheering arms up
other photographs were of dead bodies
side by side in a long neat row
as if lined up for a formal review

archer walks into the battery office
encased in a leaky poncho soaking wet
dripping rainwater on the floor
      ward was lost under the bridge
      sergeant ward is dead pretty sure
      got swept away by the flood like a twig
      pulled under the new bridge
      all clogged with trees and crap
      he is drown for sure he is
      no way anyone could survive that
captain kendall appears framed in his office doorway
chiseled granite jaw set stiff starched uniform
sergeant martineau bolts up at his chair
      what was he doing in the gosh-darn river
archer pulls a paper cup from a wall dispenser
fills it with water from the cooler by the door
      ward was drunk i mean really drunk
      he reached over the sandbag wall
      reached over to grab some piece of crap
      and before anyone could stop him
      he was yanked into the river
      swept real fast downstream
      disappearing under that bridge
      no way he could survive that

never came out the other side either
he must be stuck under the bridge
dead as far as we all can tell

wearing their leaky military issue ponchos
the two sergeants and one captain
head back to the river in the rain
it is hard not to imagine them
as walking cartoon characters
one is tall chiseled poker straight and rigid
one is short stocky quick stepping to keep up
and one is a massive block behind them
raining hard this day

chapter 8 – gather your troops

gather your troops captain
gather your troops sir
call out your battery
call them out smartly proudly
line them up
like the toy tin soldiers
you arranged in neat rows as a child
beneath the setting korean sun
snap them to attention
bark out forward march
savor the clump of many boots marching
guide your troops captain
call out the cadence
call out the cadence smartly proudly
march the battery downhill to the river
out the main gate smartly proudly
through the village past the tailor shop
past the butcher shop past the three bars
past the children who stop their play
to stand still in the dirt alley
to stare at your stern chiseled face

out on the bridge

above the still swollen river

call your troops to halt and left face

bring your troops to attention

stiff and silent order present arms

smartly and proudly salute

hold that salute in statued silence

honoring a foolish drunk sergeant

maybe honoring the hungry river

that so eagerly took the sergeant

hold that salute soldiers

without words without sounds

except for the gurgling drowning laughter

of the river below your boots

flowing under the bridge

clogged with interwoven trees and debris

maybe holding tight a sergeant's body

march your soldiers captain

march your troops sir

back through the main gate

ever smartly and proudly

the ceremony is done for a dead sergeant

tribute paid under the setting korean sun

chapter 9 – he owned the village

he owned the village
he owned the village of hasangoni
the three bars on the packed dirt main street
the one tailor shop just outside the main gate
the one butcher shop with flies on the meat
and the girls working the three bars late
he was the mayor of hasangoni
who walked easily onto the american base
to make deals with the americans
to bring greenback dollars to his village
helping his village to profit
but mostly helping him to profit

mayor kim
dressed in the best suits
always with the best tie and best overcoat
his all leather shoes were the best
his house was a small mansion
built with a lake he designed and created
circled with tall imported pine trees
always a friend of the americans

he got what they wanted without question
usually with a handshake and a smile
with the mayor the camp officers were happy
and the mayor insured that happiness
continued in the welcome he was given
that year he once came close to trouble
making a deal with the mess warrant officer
bringing the best meats for the officers
giving the poor meats to the enlisted men
the deal sealed with back room money
buying the best meats for the officers only
the warrant officer had a brick fire pit
built beside the officer's dining room
on which to grill the select steaks
the enlisted soldiers were served hot dogs
and a daily portion of tough nervy meat
the mayor profited well in those months

the lowly soldier complaints increased
the mess sergeant was investigated and
the warrant officer arrested
mayor kim acted as a simple supplier
appearing deeply shocked by the deceit
of the warrant officer and mess sergeant

against the mayor none spoke bad
he kept the contracts with colbern
to supply meat and breads and produce
he learned long ago that without papers
without signatures there is no deal
he was the mayor of hasangoni

he owned the village
he owned the village of hasangoni
the three bars on the packed dirt main street
the one tailor shop just outside the main gate
the one butcher shop with flies on the meat
and the girls working the three bars late

chapter 10 – a dismal machine gun

assigned
to a dismal machine gun position
i looked out
over a wide ice covered river
having one open place
of shallow rapids

this was an emergency bivouac
following rumors of infiltrators
rumors putting the camp into panic
everyone grabbing equipment running
throwing it into their trucks
as if the fence was already breached
we charged out the front gate
like half-witted boy scouts
eager to set tents and roast hot dogs
our convoy roared along the dirt road
creating miniature dust twisters
racing to some unknown forsaken place
where I could quickly freeze my ass off
hugging an ice cold machine gun

it was mid-winter in korea
the north wind was funneled between
mountains and over that river of ice
the gun metal was painful to touch
and no one wanted to man the gun
choosing to stand around the gun
stamping already numb feet
trying to hide from the wind

behind five extremely skinny trees
across the ice covered river
an old papa-san pedaled a rickety bicycle
slowly he moved along the dirt road
that followed the river's curve
then at the open water rapids
he got off his old rusting bicycle
rolled his white baggy papa-san pants
to just above his knees
the bicycle he lifted with some effort
placed it on his ancient shoulder
then slowly entered the knee deep rapids
with great balance crossed the river
after wading across
he rolled down his pants

got on the rickety old bicycle

pedaled off away

from us feeling frozen

dressed in our thick winter gear

chapter 11 – he counts more years

he counts more years
in the army
than first planned
now after many tours of duty
mostly lost in his memory

his face is worn
like an aged leather briefcase
his arms stay slightly bent
as if the hanger is still inside
the field jacket he wears

always a military white-walled haircut
always wearing aviator sunglasses
earning the five stripes on his uniform
a black glove conceals his left hand

hiding what remains of that unseen hand
the black glove the equal of ahab's wood leg
his glove is as visible
as his smile is not

twice sent to the vietnam jungles
once falling into a punji stake pit
the toxin smeared bamboo stakes
causing a life threatening infection

in korea one of his men had drowned
while reaching for a floating piece of wood
being sucked under the village bridge
the first soldier to die in his command

he now stands silent
on the windswept korean hill top
waiting for the instrument operator
to set up and level the theodolite

he refuses to feel the wind
as it rushes past pushing
throwing dust about
the wind tries again to move him
without success
he refuses to yield

chapter 12 – night is deathly black

this night is deathly black
a depressing affair in korea
in this damp cold foxhole
in silence i wait
i wait equally afraid
of what i can't see and what i can see
from this damp cold foxhole
that was dug two days ago
outside the camp's razor wire fence
located far outside the security fence
with my rifle loaded
and forty bullets i look without seeing
into the darkness beyond and below me
outside the camp's fence
i am a human sacrifice
trapped in this damp cold foxhole
without any option for retreat
my death might fail to alert the camp
without sound or cry from a slit throat
without a possible retreat

i wait in this foxhole knowing

my forty bullets and i are expendable

i wait in dark silence

my mind playing with the shadows

moving them up the hill toward me

the morbid darkness blurs

shapes that might be bushes or boulders

or soldiers creeping toward me

this lonely night

is a very depressing affair in korea

where everything moves and crawls

where the fence lights

are far behind me and above me

casting confusing shadows in front of me

movement on my right

i aim my rifle ready to squeeze the trigger

waiting for that movement again

i swear i see someone there

now to my left something moved yes

i sight along my rifle barrel finger on the trigger

one bullet chambered safety off

 minutes pass but the bush remains a bush

not moving as i silently watch and wait

the foretold infiltrators

are ghosts held in night shadows

i again wait in the ear throbbing silence

imagination's creatures surround me

i want to laugh hysterically

i want to scream curses on the army

i am one soldier in a foxhole

outside the razor wire fence safety

those stupid army assholes

i am one soldier in a foxhole

one rifle and forty bullets waiting

in this damp cold foxhole shaking

this night is deathly black

a depressing affair in korea

in this damp cold foxhole

in silence i wait

chapter 13 – winter morning

the winter morning
is a crisp sharp cold
we walk in the falling snow
from our barracks
uphill to the mess hall
barnes has lived his twenty years
in miami without seeing snow
or the cold here in korea

he sees the fresh flakes falling
dropping steady lazy white
from the low hanging gray sky
he runs and slides laughing unsteady
on a street covered with snow

barnes falls in his first ever snow fall
as a snowball fight starts
among the four of us now like children
making snowballs with the powdery snow
yet the real fun is watching this person
discover snow for the first time

we leave barnes rolling in the snow

then jumping up and running to join us

overjoyed with having played in the snow

but it is cold outside the wind now sweeps in

blowing snow ribbons on the street

and the mess hall will be warm

the snow is just fluffy rain to us

we who know many winters of snow

but now we are cold and hungry

chapter 14 – coordinate monuments

another bitterly cold winter day
up there to locate
known coordinate monuments
that were cement filled shell casings
buried on remote mountains tops
the local village koreans
would dig up our monuments
taking the heavy markers home
for reasons unknown to us
on that gray winter day
the snow hung above where we
searched for a monument
freezing our butts in the steady wind
nobody lived on this mountain top
a village huddled in the distant valley
dusted with powdered snow looking
like a model train landscape of gray and white

we were eating cold canned rations
chipping ice from the noodles with ham
as three little korean kids appeared

three kids watching us eat

their small noses running and crusted

wearing old patched worn clothing

we gave our crackers and bread

and hard c-ration cookies to them

yet we caught a fourth older kid

using the three kids as a decoy

while quietly unstrapping

the spare gas can from our truck

the four children ran and vanished

chapter 15 – the mess hall girl

simply known as mess hall girl
she worked in the sergeant's dining room
born in the village
surrounding the army base
daily she served food to sergeants
cleaning their tables afterwards

she was pretty
looked at by many soldiers
the girl ignored their eyes and words
not speaking keeping silent
when cleaning another table
saying nothing to them

her village of straw roofs dirt streets
and sleeping families she walked the hill
to the mess hall lights in the morning's dark
to again serve rich american soldiers
seeing around her what they brought
to her village and childhood friends

she grew up playing with girls
who were now prostitutes
living in the night of smoke drinks money
past memories of play all put aside
living in her village
she had not seen an american
until colbern was built
and then she loved a soldier
wanting to ignore his attention
walking past him in the mess hall
trying not to look at his pretty face
holding back a smile for him
she tried not to love him
yet she felt alive from his words
and she believed their love was real
he talked about oklahoma
painting her daydreams
about one day seeing tulsa
maybe being an american wife
she fought these thoughts
these dreams that wanted to be real
and on the day he left
her emptiness hurt more
than their making love

he left korea

without telling her

she was forgotten in korea

to clean tables in the mess hall

to wake each morning in her village

to walk past the rice paddies

to walk past the three bars

where childhood friends

worked now as prostitutes

in the mess hall she

would not speak to them

never speak to them again

she no longer day dreams

chapter 16 – one young lieutenant

one young lieutenant

in headquarters battery

saw himself as a movie star

performing in his mental movie

casting himself and his southern rebel driver

in a korean rat patrol television series

wearing australian style hats

one side tacked up

jeep driving off the base

flying skull and cross-bone flags

from the twin radio whip antennas

korea became just a movie set

for him and his driver

he was quietly allowed to play his fantasy

blazing out the gate pirate flags flapping

until the day he was heard speaking

of the blacks at colbern

as ignorant coons

he was quietly transferred to the border

leaving behind a conforming jeep driver

who never displayed the hats and flags again

chapter 17 – is he hiding

is he hiding
his homosexuality so well
that maybe
he is not

it is hard
to be sure that he is
just as hard
to be sure he is not

yet he did
for a short time
see the korean mess hall girl
who worked there silently

he told
stories about them
having sex
how she cried that it hurt

yet again

stories could not resolve

the known certainty

or equally known uncertainty

although

neither seemed to matter

to anybody else

in the camp

the truth

about him

exposed or hidden

was pretty much unimportant

chapter 18 – the army and this draftee

the army and this draftee
we were never a well matched couple
never did fit with korea either
yet it was a not to be forgotten experience
still to this day my having dreams
and nightmares about that year
feeling like one of few blacks
that had a college degree
most blacks talking as if barely
graduated from high school
some almost proud of ignorance
uneducated and violent and stupid
feeling embarrassed by them
becoming the battery clerk
to prove my not being them
my duties became a matter of pride
typing without error morning reports
staying one step ahead of office requests
calling out attention when captain kendall
entered the building each morning
snapping to military attention

saluting before anyone else

refusing be the typical army black

in their drinking and whoring

the evenings did not drag me

to the hill top club with the others

or getting into drunken fights there

my nights were not spent in whoring

instead remaining in the barracks

drinking a six pack of cola

that one year

in korea seemed the longest year

daily typing meaningless papers or letters

and morning reports for a meaningless camp

packed with nuclear missiles and drunks

rednecks and venereal disease

i stayed to myself

or with a few white friends

avoiding the loud blacks and

avoiding the ignorant southern rednecks

never being sure which was worse

chapter 19 – in a black night

in a black night
the darkest night
miles away from anywhere
after the alert flashed
of another north korean threat
we packed our trucks
and loaded our missiles
to again play hide and seek
with the anticipated infiltrators

in the black night
i walked our perimeter
in that total darkness
so dense that straining my eyes
i could see nothing
there was nothing to see
the sky earlier a gray painted ceiling
had turned coal black without stars or moon
without house lamps or village glow seen
with only gravity showing
what was up or down

distance was known by counting steps

then walking back the same number steps

trusting that an about-face turn was true

my ears rang and buzzed

trying to gather any sounds

where a dark shape

became a tree on my right

when just beyond another faint blur

came a dark slow moving shadow

approaching as a misty ghost

to where i stood

hearing my heart beating

pounding in my ears

the dark shadow advanced

moving now in front of me

feeling adrenaline fueled anticipation

the shape became corporal sung

a korean soldier assigned to colbern

also on guard duty but having strayed

passing in front of me

close enough for me to touch

yet i remained still as stone

daring not to startle sung

seeing he carried a loaded rifle

in both hands ready to use
sung never saw me that night
he was a specter passing before me
unaware of my being there inches away
he continued walking slowly
again swallowed by the night

i remained as motionless
as the tree beside me
my rifle held tight across my chest
my eyes only following Sung
until he vanished
no longer hearing his footsteps
in a night so dark
we could walk unseen past another

the thought came to me later
had i also walked
unaware past someone
if i had reached out that night
would i have by chance touched
standing beside me in the dark
something warm and breathing

chapter 20 – know about doing patrol

i know about doing patrol
freezing in the winter night hours
feeling the wind blow through
sweeping down the mountain
and then summer sweating buckets
swatting at moths the size of bats
fighting off clouds of mosquitos
i know well enough about doing patrol
nobody need tell me about duty
or what a flat faced north korean looks like

let me tell you about that day
we were getting ready
to walk our mountain patrol
when martineau waddles in talking
about north gooks moving toward colbern
and for us to stay alert
which just got some of us all jumpy
we went out in the early light
with everyone quiet and alert
we saw nothing the whole time

maybe frightening a few birds
until a good ways through the patrol
when among some trees i see this gook
standing still and holding a rifle
pointing it straight at me

i raise my weapon
snapping off a few rounds
and one shot clocks him good
he spins and drops
then all hell breaks loose
everyone going completely nuts
yelling and ducking behind cover
their rifles ready for some big battle
      what the hell happened flint
      what are you shooting at
kubicki yells running back to me
i says a gook was set to fire on us
so we advanced rifles ready
to where the gook was on the ground
bleeding from the shoulder
where my bullet hit him
the bullet went clean through
kubicki called the situation in to the camp

as two guys worked to stop the bleeding
we waited for the medics there
without much talking just watching
the old gook and us waiting

the next day
i was called in for an investigation
i told them
that the gook was going to pop me
there was no time to ask what to do
i swear on a double stack of holy bibles
they said i shot an old village papa-san
hunting rabbits for his family
he was hunting rabbits my butt
he is a damned gook sympathizer
yet i get written up
shooting without authorization
but the whole incident gets covered up
with the papa-san getting paid hush money

i get yanked from doing patrols
they say i am too dangerous
the brass actually said i am too dangerous
maybe in their eyes i am

but i did enjoy being labeled

too dangerous by the top brass

of that i am proud

chapter 21 – bowlegged

bowlegged he walks
determined ever bent over
with a boxer's nose broken
looking like a staircase
on a face that showed
scars of fights years ago

his face is nature's portrait
of what tough looks like
in basic training he was placed
in front of forty green men
to be their platoon leader
and whether by nature or fear
his men obeyed when he barked
they obeyed without question

in korea
he is made sergeant
well before others with more time
the army wanted to keep him

he is a product of chicago

having learned early

what a massive fist

could do to flesh and bone

having felt

what a sharp knife

could do to skin and face

yet somehow somewhere

he also learned compassion

           and his men knew this

chapter 22 – the orphan visit

in two buses the children arrived
from seoul for the day
invited for an easter celebration
two military buses bringing the orphans

small beautiful creatures stepping
out of a dark green vehicles
greeted by the our camp director
and nervous american soldiers

the children came for one day
with their orphanage nuns
as teachers and mothers to them all
guiding them gently into the building

for their practiced traditional dances
wearing costumes from a time
before the war and americans
the children had songs to sing
ancient folk tunes

from honored generations past
taught to them by the nuns
to sing for the american soldiers
the smallest children looked around

happy with words forgotten
these children came full of a happiness
that time and place would erode
they were led to the mess hall

fed a full meal with milk and dessert
with soldiers serving the meals
and cleaning the tables afterwards
always affected by the small faces

that looked up to them from large chairs
appearing lost in those chairs
there then was an easter egg hunt
on the grassy uphill slope

that led up to the helipad
the nuns helping the smallest children
to find candy or a small toy
each child held a woven basket

and with full baskets their visit ended
given more presents of clothing books games
they were loaded onto their buses
the happy children waving through windows

as the buses drove out the main gate
and they were gone
the buildings were then suddenly quiet
lit red-orange by the setting sun

the soldiers drifted away silently
maybe trying to keep the visit real
the camp filled with an emptiness
some soldiers walked to the barracks

others down the hill to the club
soon the streets were empty
      and like the children before it
      this one special day was gone

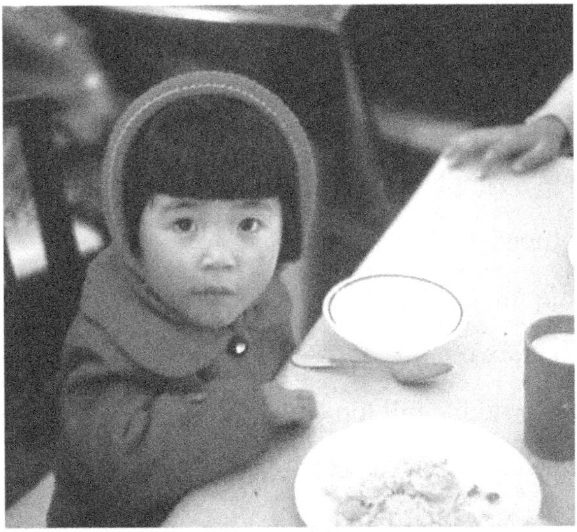

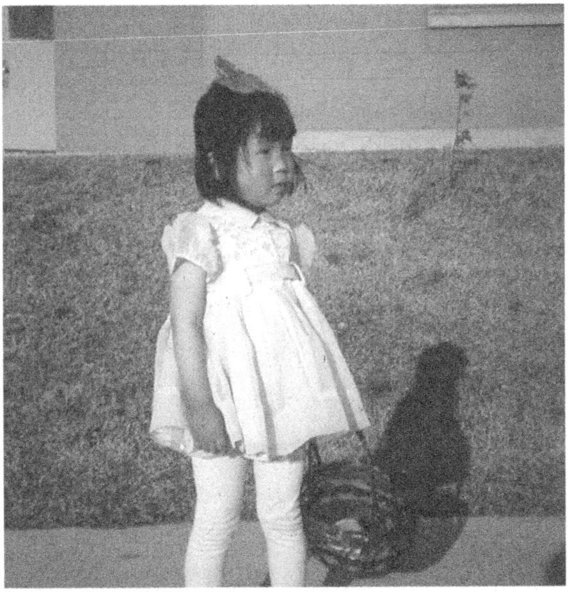

chapter 23 – six months

his first six months
he lived in an endless march of days
six long months of thinking
of his wife in maryland
for his first six months
he went only to the hill top club
there to drink with a friend or two
to toast the passage of another day
his drinking helped to forget
the draft notice that arrived one day
seeming so long in the past now
and about the miscarriage that night
and the twins they lost that night
forever the army's fault
in his mind and heart
at the club the memory dimmed
he would be faithful
that one full year away
just one year in korea
true to his wife and his honor
but his first six months

became a much longer time
with thoughts of his distant wife
he then stayed one night
with a village girl

his days
after that one night
were filled with his guilt
from which there was no escape
betrayal always sat by his side
he lived his first six months
proud of his faithfulness
and his last six months
tormented by that one village night

chapter 24 – rush to somewhere

we throw our equipment into trucks
scramble the camp
hook up the missile carriers and launchers

storm out the main gate
drive to a secret destination
located unknown miles somewhere

to hide there from enemy infiltrators
miles of swirling dust and diesel fumes
created by our drab green trucks

the scenery flashing by
all a jerky bumping jumble
of mountains rice paddies

and tiny villages disappearing in dust
with children beside the road watching
we do not pause in our rush to somewhere

going deeper into the mountains and valleys
we arrive coughing with our nose and ears
dust clogged our red rimmed eyes tearing

ending at our isolated hiding place
the patrols and sentry posts quickly set
razor wire unrolled from the trucks

uncoiled with heavy gloves
circling our camp perimeter
machine guns and trip flares are placed

the launcher is set up and stabilized
one missile hangs from the launcher arm
with a sixty kiloton nuclear warhead

painted an innocent dull olive green
as the crew completes the firing sequence
and the missile is now ready

for a flaming launch
somewhere within range
people go about their day

unaware that many miles away

hidden between ancient mountains

our missile with a nuclear warhead

is pointing at them

ready

      ready

           ready

chapter 25 – he was rotund

he was rotund
always happy belly laughing
showing his chipped front tooth
wearing huge army issue glasses

he more waddled
than walked when walking
being happy was enough reason
to be happy for him
smiling his chipped tooth smile

he would push
those huge black frame glasses
higher up the bridge of his nose
with one thick pudgy finger

he had married
before his korea assignment
and being married sustained
his level of happiness in korea

he received
further transfer orders
that sent him
to the demilitarized zone
there to fill a specialty vacancy

and his rotund body
was sent home
to his widow
before another two korean months
had been fully forgotten

he was rotund
always happy belly laughing

chapter 26 – throwing stones

a small group of children
from the village threw stones
at the solitary soldier's back
some hitting his back
but bouncing off harmless

he continued walking along
the earthen wall separating
water flooded rice paddies
knowing that little children
were throwing stones at him

he was unconcerned
by the few harmless pebbles
that bounced off his field jacket
he understood their reason
for he was the foreign intruder

he accepted being pelted
with small stones
by those children because

he knew he would be throwing

the same stones

if he were one of them

he continued walking along

the earthen wall separating

water flooded rice paddies

knowing that little children

were throwing stones at him

chapter 27 – day is going away

day is going away
the hurting orange light going away
no humans here in my shop
no sounds i hear
except my gentle panting
my slight wheezing
my endless scratching
my cautious nervous twitching
the shop is now empty
no more bright lights
the dangerous humans gone
see the table covered
with many tasty meats
tasty gray octopus hanging limp
by the dirty front window
of this butcher shop
my years have grown fat
grown bigger than cat
but cat is only found in a pot
i feel no sorrow for cat
my long life has lived in this shop

defending my meat shop against

the other diseased ones

their short brittle whiskers

and dull sickly damaged tails

and dirty broken little claws

my body bigger than them

too big to challenge or hurt

they feel my sharp claws

they know how deeply

my teeth sink into their flesh

to enjoy the taste of their blood

before my feast tonight

i clean beautiful hairless tail

and then chew on tasty red meat

but a human stands outside

his dark green skin still

he watches me eat

and i watch him unafraid

he does not frightened me

let him watch outside

the dirt smeared glass

that is between us protecting me

i eat my meal

until he walks away

leaving me alone in my butcher shop

where the darkness comforts me

to eat some squid next

then i am full and will sleep curled

and dream of my good life here

chapter 28 – after his discharge

he re-enlisted in the army
two years after his first discharge
after surviving two years unemployed
in new york two years of begging for work
he re-enlisted to wear the uniform again
arriving at camp colbern in korea

his presence irritated those draftees
he had re-enlisted for what they hated
becoming the object of their hatred
this they refused to understand
this they refused to accept
declaring unemployment was better

his was a presence of what they secretly feared
that haunted their darkest night hours
that same as he they may not find a job
and in humiliation do what he did
re-enlisting so as to survive
and again become what they hated

he rests on his bunk
reading a magazine when
some draftees return drunk from the club
and gather around his bunk
with angry words try to push him
becoming their hatred for the army

to his face they yell
they begin jabbing with their fists
as a street fighter he is ready
and this excite the draftees
wanting him to fight back
they rush him yet he gets free
running into the latrine

they swarm after him their blood up
he stands alone in the latrine
 to slam his elbow back
shattering the single glass window
grabbing the largest glass shard
waving it at them

he stands facing a now silent pack
holding his weapon with both hands bleeding

pointing it at the men blocking the door
at first in triumph they feel
with his charge into the latrine
now they see his glass sword

       come on all of you
       come on get cut good
       who wants the first cut
       how about you now
       not so brave are we now
       messing with this new yorker
       who is ready to cut you all

the draftees stand without speaking
their early words and threats gone
they disappear one by one
until their leader alone remains
the draftee facing the enlistee

       you are completely insane
       yeah i know

the draftee leaves the doorway
returns to his bunk nothing more said
an army base is a strange place
where unpredictable things happen

in time the draftee and the enlistee

become friends

chapter 29 – maybe twice late

maybe twice late
into the night hours
he will play solitaire
maybe one game
as if that game were an interruption
to the shuffle of worn cards
the endless shuffle of the cards
tapping down the cards on the table
shuffle tap shuffle tap

staring blankly far away
staring into his own nowhere
he might play one disconnected
game of solitaire getting it over
getting it out of the way
getting back to the shuffle and tap
all night alone at the small table
shuffle tap shuffle tap

disconnected staring into that nowhere
sometimes at midnight he would

leave his cards in his foot locker

to go up onto the helipad

there to play his saxophone

to an uninterested audience of stars

lonely callings in the night

then back to shuffling and tapping

late into the night without words

he had been in vietnam

eight months led to his breakdown

then his transfer to rehab in korea

his experience ever visible

shuffle tap shuffle tap shuffle tap

chapter 30 – no hatred

no hatred did i feel
for the white soldiers
after martin was assassinated
by a white man's bullet killed

we wanted the white guys to stay away
leave me and my brothers alone
his death meant nothing to them
his murder meant everything to us

his death was inevitable they said
after his speeches it was expected
their eyes said what did you expect
he gave us blacks hope

their eyes said to us that
his life and words meant nothing
just another black making trouble
just getting what he was asking for

we ignored the white soldiers
seeing in them partners in his death
just racists of different degrees
walking around laughing and telling jokes

unconcerned about what his death meant
to us trapped in a white world
where a white guy kills a black guy
dying on a cheap motel balcony

we were once american soldiers together
but one bullet made two camps
one of black and one of white
where skin color became a solid wall

we wore dark sunglasses
when on duty and in the mess hall
defiantly adding black leather gloves
silently declaring black power in the camp

my afro was not in their code of conduct
nor was the black power we talked
our attitude screamed keep away
unless you understand and regret his death

sergeants and officers they left me alone

not any warning given to me

they left me alone

letting my hostile attitude fester

we blacks did our daily assignments

carrying a large black chip

daring someone to knock it off

withdrawing into our black brotherhood

so maybe for a time yes

there was hatred for the whites

maybe for a time i gave in

to the same blind ignorant racism

the same worthless racist hatred

that killed martin luther king

chapter 31 – springtime in korea

springtime in korea

was an unexpected fragrant experience

with the smell of fermented waste

hanging on every warming breeze

the season of raw animal waste

being spooned on the rice paddies

when farmers would all spread

the foul smelling brew

brown and lumpy and watery

with an army helmet attached

securely to a pole

making a large ladle

the small farmer then pulled

behind a massive water buffalo

plowing the awakening soil

mixing in the ripe aged waste

for a year it would stew

in the village collective pit

farmer then wading knee deep all day

without protective leg coverings
walking with his animal
plowing the dirt
seemingly immune to whatever
was living in that toxic mix

one day i walked an earthen wall
between two rice paddies
the earthen wall having
a narrow footpath along the top
with flooded rice paddies on both sides

my left foot slid down
the side of the earth dike
into the mucky diseased water
my entire boot disappeared into
the muck to half way up my shin
i instantly pulled my leg out
pouring water from my boot
and rinsing my leg with canteen water

by evening my leg had a nasty rash
inflamed and burning red going
on sick-call where the medics

applied antibacterial cremes and injections

a full week of washing and cremes

to kill what infected this american leg

this is my memory of spring in korea

chapter 32 – eternal mayor

eternal mayor of his village
promoter and caretaker of his village
winning the every election
he always campaigned unopposed
his smiling face cemented all business
with each new commanding american officer
acquiring whatever the americans needed
delivered with a smile they quickly learned
his overcoat was expensively crafted
fashionable in the cold korean winter
only wearing suits of the finest materials
sculpted by his tailor in the village shop

the laundry service was his to offer
as was the cleaning of the officer quarters
as was the shoe repair and shine shop
as were the services of the village prostitutes
always present to make a new deal
or to polish an existing deal
the mayor could own the largest house
on a hill overlooking his village

but the camp medical officer reported
that venereal disease in the village
was higher than military medical limits
and the village was declared off-limits

the main gate of the camp stayed closed
the village girls were suddenly without income
at night the three bars sat empty
out of business without soldier's money
the mayor told his girls
to gather at the camp gate
to loudly shout and scream at the guards
protesting the nightly empty beds
some girls threw rocks and bottles
and the mayor sent a message
for some at the front gate
to begin climbing the chain links

one sergeant ordered the girls to stop
or his men would open fire there
yet the mayor knew none would shoot
and he arrived that moment to bring order
the girls were quiet as to the gate he walked
where the colonel waited to meet the mayor

and with the medical officer

and medics following they talked

with a handshake and a smile

the girls would receive medication

so the gates would open to resume business

with posted photos and names of the clean girls

the medics provided weekly examinations

the camp gates stayed free of protest

his village girls were doing business again

and he was again elected mayor

chapter 33 – year of my command

we were not touched by combat
during the year of my command
although five north koreans did come
to within three miles of colbern
before being found and removed

we never did know
what their intentions were
the camp was put on high alert
taking our missiles out of reach
as required by evacuating the camp

but all the combat in korea
was unknown to the world
with all eyes focused on vietnam
that year of their tet invasion

our conflicts were small
along the border with the fights
never becoming headlines
so my year at colbern came

and went without casualties

i held my breath for one year
sometimes now thinking back then
feeling a chill seeing five ghosts
thinking of those north koreans
so close to my camp

what they could have done
with our nine nuclear warheads

chapter 34 – smash his hand

the soldier tried one night
to smash his hand
hoping this would get him out
loathing the army and colbern
from his first korean winter day
from the arrival of his draft notice

that first korean winter
drove inescapable cold into him
he once placed
on the window sill overnight
a can of soda that with the
morning light was frozen solid

his right hand he tried breaking
two months into that winter
being drunk enough
going into the latrine
where he faced the block wall
made a good solid fist
and starting punching the wall

punching that block wall
with the hatred the drunk set free

he would not later remember
it at first hurting fierce
then feeling nothing but his purpose
seeing blood spattered spots
and streaks on the wall

he felt less with each punch
       you have to hit harder
       you do not belong here
       you have to get out
he did think there should be pain
but his mind only saw a drunk soldier
slamming his fist into a solid wall

two soldiers found him there
restraining him until others came
and medics wrapped his hand
two surgeries set the hand right
leaving scars and some stiffness
a souvenir of his time in korea

pounding his fist

against a cinder block wall

did not get him discharged

did not let him leave korea

chapter 35 – whiskey and cola

whiskey and cola
would ease him into the night
one swallow of whiskey
two gulps of cola after

he would sit in silence
in the dim barrack bay light
the orange glow of a cigarette
flaring between drinks

one swallow of whiskey
two gulps of cola after
slowing his southern drawl
when he spoke at all

maybe a curse infused sentence
concerning the army or korea
or maybe it was a distant memory
of the good days driving hell bent

some big eighteen wheel rig

back home along an interstate

or a lonely back country road

going to or away from home

one swallow of whiskey

two gulps of cola after

his cigarette tip flaring bright orange

as the only signal of his presence

whiskey and cola

would ease him into the night

chapter 36 – said the captain

said the captain

expect an attack

during the next few days

said the captain

they are planning

to destroy our missile bunkers

green berets then came to test our security

their silent night arrival secret

getting easily into our bunkers

our security failed their test

and if it had been the enemy

radioactive vapor we would be

drifting between those mountains

and floating over rice paddies

our patrols were then increased

foxholes were dug in defendable spots

our guards to walk the fence in teams

additional high intensity lamps were placed

more trip flares were wired

more dog patrols scheduled

and guards added inside the bunkers

then we waited deep in anxiety

for the anticipated assault asking

what if one infiltrator makes the bunker

it is late evening

when the night is ripped open

with the near sound of gunfire

and camp sirens screaming loud

lights blink on turning the night into day

and everyone is running serious crazy

grabbing helmets and web belts cursing

slamming locker doors charging

from their barracks to the armory

where freeman is handing out rifles

as we run through the armory building

each grabbing two clips of bullets

i run up the long hill

to a dark and damp bunker

half sunk down in the ground

half built up with sandbag walls

covered with a plywood and sandbag roof

there i charge through the narrow entrance

breathing fast heart hard pounding

alone

waiting

looking out through the slit openings
with dripping moisture the bunker smells
of oiled canvas damp earth and i wait
alone
come on
come on
where is everyone already
then three others arrive at the bunker
out of breath without words where
we all crouch at the slit openings
in the musty sand bags
we look into the ground hugging fog
moving about as if given life
a single searchlight sweeps the fence line
the sirens stop their screaming
letting silence again fill the night
it is black in the bunker
a cold heavy black
with dampness thick and smothering
i can see my breath and i adjust my helmet
to shield my eyes from the searchlight glare
we hear muffled shouts eerie and faint
sounding far away muted with night's haze
then more shouts louder and more urgent

then quiet sounding worse than the shouts

something is happening whispers thompson

be sure your safety is off he says

with a bullet in the chamber he says

see anything jankowsky he says

nothing yet sir i whisper

i cannot see much through the narrow slits

mind creates images of north koreans

creeping up soundlessly to my bunker

ready to charge inside

or roll a grenade among us

the cold fingers of panic i feel upon me

aware that a korean soldier could be

on the other side

of this sandbag wall

waiting deathly quiet

one sandbag's width from me

    in the darkness

    i listen

    and wait

chapter 37 – one morning patrol

on one morning patrol
we walked a new mountain trail
and entered a burial site
fairly high on the mountain side

the burial site was quiet and calm
with two large oval earthen mounds
side by side on a level grassy floor
surrounded with wispy pines

the mounds rested there
circled with carved stone statues
that faced the burial mounds
standing as silent guardians

it was said that the higher
a person's position in life
the higher up the mountain
that body would be placed

so it still remains for me
the most calming place
where i felt filled with peace
long remembered to this day

is there an afterlife
that we go to when each we die
none can know or say for sure
those mounds seemed to say
it doesn't really matter

chapter 38 – one year filled

one year filled
with killings back home
during that year in korea
martin luther king was killed
bobby kennedy was killed
good men both gone

with martin dead
i withdrew into myself
and into my black brothers
trying to accept and forgive
as the camp became acidic
one camp became two camps

of black soldiers or white soldiers
each enclosed into themselves
as sergeant i was expected to be neither
but as a black sergeant i knew
watching my brothers stew in their anger
boiling up to the surface
angry silence clawing deep inside

the hill top club became a bonfire

wanting a single match to ignite

blacks this side and whites that side

ready to burst into raging flames

skin color dividing the barracks

barely contained without spreading

sergeants were not black or white

always expected to be army green

we turned disorder into order

forever in control of the troops

yet as a black sergeant

i knew where i would stand

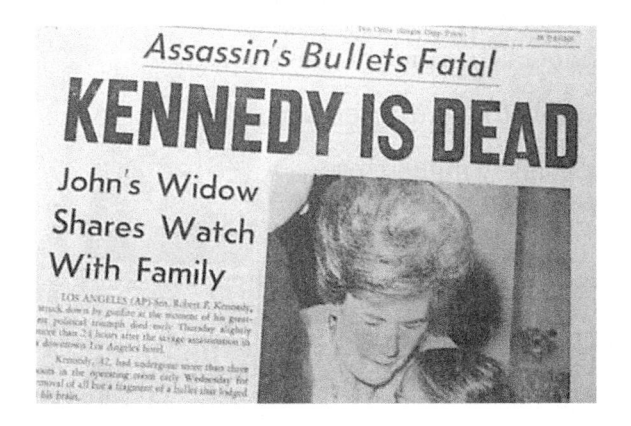

Assassin's Bullets Fatal
KENNEDY IS DEAD
John's Widow Shares Watch With Family

chapter 39 – new assignment

the lieutenant's new assignment
is to exercise the soldiers
about which he admits knowing nothing
he orders a two mile run each afternoon
under a low hanging orange sun
he assembles the troops
all wearing white t-shirts
with fatigue pants and army boots
not designed for running
they gather facing a still blazing sun
when he calls attention
and marches them out the front gate
looking more like prisoners than soldiers
they begin shuffling in double time
he sets a standard military pace
watching the mostly out of shape soldiers
he thinks please no injuries or deaths
he takes the road beside the river
where sergeant ward drown
he calls out an airborne ranger cadence
thinking a battle cadence will inspire them

        i want to be an airborne ranger
        i want to go to vietnam
        i want to be an airborne ranger
        i want to kill some vietcong

village children gather bewildered
as the soldiers run up hill
in korea they run up or down a hill
he stops calling cadence
the sun dissolves into a mountain
they turn to run back their breathing strained
there is no talk just the sand-paper scraping
of boots along the dusty road
when back in sight of their camp
he starts calling cadence loudly
they shuffle past the main gate
hoping that nobody will throw-up
sweating dripping cursing breathless
worn out from the short run

after one week the daily runs stop

chapter 40 – the dust of texas

he spoke with a haziness
as if the dust of texas
had followed him to korea
clinging to his face and hands
dusting his vocal cords
with a fine gravel powdering his words
as a spoken tumble weed rolling past

he was a giant by all measure
a mechanic in the motor pool
days filled with spark plugs and grease
evenings filled with beer and whiskey
double shots at the hill top club
with his best friend mouse
over time they seemed as one person

theirs a mutt and jeff friendship
as one tall and slow
the other short and twitchy
both working in the motor pool
with each sometimes ending

the other's sentences as if scripted

until one night

when heavily fueled with booze

mizell turned on his best friend

who was a tough scrappy type

yet the big clunky texan

easily beat up his friend

ending their friendship

first found then lost in korea

chapter 41 – recreation of choice

heavy drinking nightly
was my recreation of choice
for this lone star texan

martin luther king was shot
the black soldiers became quiet
what i would call angry quiet

before the shooting
they sang together in the latrine
the block walls giving a nice echo

after king their singing stopped
they gathered in small groups
talking and watching us white guys

can't say i was upset
about him getting shot like he did
can't say it was unexpected

i always spoke my mind freely

when drunk i spoke maybe too freely
not remembering later all that i said

that night i got into a little debate
with one of the blacks in my barracks
he was usually a nice guy

i asked him what would happen
if he went around the country
preaching what king preached

being drunk and all fired up
what i said after that
i do not seem to recall

but i do well remember
seeing the guys gathered around
suddenly pushed aside
like moses parting the red sea

in slow motion i saw taylor
burst through looking mean
with one hand he lifted me

by the throat pinning me
against the barracks wall
my feet not touching the floor

injustice he lived as a black
boiled into anger did fill his eyes
his large right arm pulled back

his big fist held ready hesitating
i hung silent frozen in my fear
like marble statues we remained

until he exhaled softly
seeming to expel that anger
letting me drop to the floor

he walked away without
speaking walking back through
the silent crowd to his bunk

where he sat in the dark
with a glowing cigarette
holding his head in his hands

they told me the next day
that i had used the nigger word
that pushed taylor beyond rage

he was a psychology graduate
who had every reason to hurt
a drunk texan but he did not

chapter 42 – memories still remain

memories still remain
of my year at colbern
sixty-eight was an awful year
for those who were there
somewhere in their heads lie
wanted and unwanted memories
waiting for that perfect moment
to come out of hiding

memories still remain
of the pueblo taken at sea
her crew thrown into a gook prison
increased shooting along the border
talk of war whispered daily
wanted and unwanted memories
some as simply as kimchi
and riding in a three-quarter ton
with two katusas who ate kimchi
the night before stinking up
that small truck so bad
i wanted to throw them out

or the time we were ordered
to dig foxholes outside the camp
really screwing our guys
on the wrong side of the fence
being dead meat if we were attacked
some idiot thought that was a good idea
after a day or two we dug new foxholes
within the safe perimeter of the fence

or once going through a monsoon
with weeks of endless pouring rain
building a sandbag wall to keep
the village from washing away
and sergeant ward going downstream
bobbing up and down like a cork
getting sucked under the bridge
to drown without his body ever found
what a way to go stuck under a bridge
the search team found cows and ox
and pigs tangled but no sergeant

or memories of an officer being shot at
by a contract guard along the fence
the lieutenant found the guard sleeping

who awoke and fired at the lieutenant
missing the officer with a shotgun
how can you miss with a shotgun

i remember when we scrambled the base
hearing that enemy soldiers had crossed
and i jumped into the communications truck
with the missile launcher behind me
and i somehow made a wrong turn
with the missile launcher following me into
a tiny village where we could not turn around
i radioed for help and got chewed out real good

and the time i thought i would be killed
by an angry mob when my friend
accidentally hit a papa-san
while driving near walker hill
the old man was okay after a short rest
and i remember movies in the little theater
the folding chairs and windows blackened
i remember nightly losing money with friends
in the old slot machines at the hill top club
and lots of lonely times writing letters
about the bitterly cold winter

the endlessly hot humid summer

the days and nights wasted

i remember all too well sometimes

chapter 43 – bust me

they wanted to bust me
for sure the sergeants did
especially martineau wanted to
making my life a living hell
he hated pot smoking hippies
calling me flower child pothead and
the hippie from san francisco
my existing bothered him
 my living somehow challenged
his military way of life
his many years in the army
his fighting wars and killing people

screw his wars and bombs and guns
happier i would be outside the army
or not being at that godforsaken camp
where martineau daily got on my case
i became friends with the medics
who were the best source of pot
and the drugs soldiers used to forget
as the only way to survive the army

one medic would sometimes join me

on the helipad sharing weed into the night

hearing the guys at the hill top club

getting toasted and fighting

yelling and beating up on each other

while i smoked my pot on the hill

listening to them cursing and swearing

stumbling drunk back to the barracks

 pausing to puke their guts

on the street or on themselves

yet the army provided booze on base

while pot was some big offense

i listened to the night

watched the stars filling the sky

smoked my grass in peace

and dream about being home

chapter 44 – trice is dead

    trice is dead
    volunteered to be
    a helicopter pilot
    over vietnam shot down

    trice wanted not
    a surveyor to be
    jungle stomping
    to find the vietcong

    trice bought fully
    the dream of flight
    flying high above
    real bed for sleep

    trice we said
    the army wants
    chopper pilots to
    fill empty death seats

trice laughed at

more meat

for the grinder

now trice is dead

chapter 45 – dummies

those officers were dummies
they came to me for everything
had to tell them what to do
how to set coordinates
the best spot to set the camp
where to place the sentry posts
where to set up the missile
a bunch of dummies

i was the sole black officer
the soul black officer
they were lucky that i was there

the colonel was a bigger dummy
so i nicknamed him the mummy
he had nothing to say or add
about how to make things work
they were jealous of me
i would have been jealous of me
if i were one of those dummies
and mayor kim was taking them

to the cleaners every day

whenever he came through the gate

he owned the village and it's people

and i would say he owned colbern

bunch of dummies

was i the only one who saw this

chapter 46 – very somber mountain

that brown and green mountain
was a very somber mountain
forever hulking behind colbern
an ancient backdrop filling the east
a rock and dirt buddha uncaring
of the tiny men moving below
the mountain blocked every sunrise
until after mid-morning
casting a solid shadow across the valley
where the night's chill found shelter
to hide and crouch from the bright sun
until it emerged throwing light and warmth
the silent mountain secretly cuddled
a small brook of clear water
its flow slowed by deep pools
stepped with miniature waterfalls
tripping over the rocky ledges
worthy of being in local tour books

i stood by a deep clear pool
looking out to the valley below

where a rich spring green carpet

lay a mosaic of rice paddies

beyond which in farther distance

was seen the han river

and receding again beyond that

rose a jumble of blue-gray humps

of mountains taller than this mountain

with one full day to climb

i ascended less than halfway

before having to start back down

taking back the memory of a brook

seeming untouched by human ways

and i would be disappointed

for not seeing korea

from that mountain's very crown

chapter 47 – the helipad

the helipad is cluttered
packed with our trucks
and our missile launcher
and communication trucks
and sergeant missile tubes

and jeeps and kitchen truck
all jammed onto the helipad
this is the idea
of our new full bird colonel
there to use the helipad

as a staged mission so ordered
to pretend being on a mission
rather than an real field exercise
the camp's vehicles
the missiles and launchers

are now parked on the helipad
doing an exercise in make believe
occupying the entire helipad

under a clear crystal blue sky
when swooping over the hilltops

tightly hugging the landscape
at just above treetop level
appear two large helicopters
moving fast for the helipad
like angry hornets they buzz over

the landing pad now filled with trucks
they take turns skimming the soldiers
churning huge dust tornados
they have arrived in secret
their flight plan never published

for they are carrying
new fresh nuclear warheads
the pilots show their anger
by repeat buzzing of the pretend army
causing soldiers to run wildly

caught in the dust storm turbulence
grabbing loose gear being blown
holding caps and helmets tightly

scrambling into trucks and jeeps
creating an olive green traffic jam

in a tightly packed frenzy
vehicles are barely off the helipad
as one helicopter makes a quick landing
the second one remains circling guarding
the warheads are rotated out

old for new at a frantic pace
helicopter blades are kept spinning
at just below lift speed
the engines never shut down
the mission is done

and blade speed increases
the helicopter lifts to emerge suddenly
from within it's own dust cloud
ascending to join the second helicopter
both disappearing over the mountain

a slowly settling dust cloud remains
hanging over the empty helipad
allowing the quiet to return

the colonial does not repeat the exercise

only the smell of fertilized rice paddies

is left to fill the air

chapter 48 – weapons

weapons were my specialty
trained and assigned to maintain
and secure our weapons
at first finding it ironic
with me being jewish
put in charge of weapons

but then why not a jew
when no other people
had more first hand experience
with weapons through the ages
when no other people
know the feel of bullets

weapons were my specialty
although during a field exercise
we practiced firing
one of three machine guns
shooting into a hillside
when the hot tracers
ignited the hillside's dry grass

where pale smoke flashed into flames

and more soldiers came over to watch

we all watched helpless

as the hillside burned

too large for us to control

but the fire quickly burned out

having consumed all available grass

yet never going over the hill

so ended our machine gun practice

using tracer bullets

chapter 49 – after the monsoon

after the monsoon rains ended
we heard of a tank crew drowning
while trying to cross the imgin river
first refusing to upon seeing
the high rushing water of that river
the young lieutenant in command
ordered the tank sergeant and his crew
to drive through the high flood water
when half way across the tank swamped
quickly filling with water
the tank disappeared under the flood
drowning the sergeant and his crew
unable to scramble from their metal trap
where they remained entombed
until the river level dropped
does anyone remember this
of a tank crew drowning

chapter 50 – patrolling the green mountain

patrolling the green mountain
as a young second lieutenant
stunned by the view down
at our buried missile bunkers
circled with three bands
of perimeter fence each
crowned with razor wire
the machine gun towers
the patrol dogs walking

what am i doing here

after reading the army manual
on terms of engagement
it was clear why we were there
one order prohibited
firing at an enemy aircraft
unless its bombay doors were open
and heading towards us
clearly we were the tripwire
the canary in the coal mine

other memories flash by

the long ride on dirt roads to seoul

the women along side the road

with babies on their backs

making gravel

from large rocks

using hammers

as part of a paving project

another time

i had to use

the handbrake on the truck

after fording a river

during a field exercise

frozen black potatoes

horrible reconstituted milk

served in aluminum pitchers

one solid month

never going above minus thirty

and that full month

of continuous rain and mud

that day our supply truck

overturned in the river

drowning some civilians

and the locals

stealing supplies

on a regular basis

one of our guard dogs

leaving bloody footprints

in the icy snow around

the missile bunker perimeter

teaching a houseboy

how to play chess

and helping a warrant officer

build the brick barbecue

behind the officer quarters

and drinking pitchers of martinis

after duty with the enlisted guys

lastly i remember

my short timer's calendar

telling me it was time

to go home

chapter 51 – scribbled notes

i kept some scribbled notes
from the korean border
where my tour of duty started
after the pueblo was boarded
that winter of bitter cold
well below zero most nights
warm bunkers did not exist
it was dangerous to be outside
targets for north koreans snipers
eager to pull the trigger
they were like ghosts to us
showing up everywhere
trying to penetrate the
fence and ambush us
they sent special hunter-killer
five man units across the border
or putting american flags on their
positions across the border
trying to make us think
they were american positions

fence duty was boring
and spooky all at the same time
few of us slept
but the katusa boys did
sorry little rich boys
from wealthy families
not wanting their little boys
going to vietnam
buying safety with us

the cooks would send
hot coffee and hot potato soup
on the really cold nights
but by the time it reached us
and we got back in our holes
it would be frozen solid
so if we heard any noise
in front of our fence
we would throw
the frozen soup first
and then a hand grenade
to seal the deal
as payback for their easter ambush
of the guards going to panmunjom

and the train wreck shootings
when they killed
some of our guys
but we are not allowed
to talk about that either
accidental discharge of a weapon
or training accident
became the cover words

i saw a few guys
go psycho while on the border
a couple who just ended it
overdosing on whatever handy
some left early with combat fatigue
some got to rotate home
and some did the trip home
in a body bag

for five months
i could count on one hand
how many times
i slept between two sheets
in a real bed
most times sleeping

on the bunker's concrete floor

sometimes in a sleeping bag

with a pistol in my hand

and a round in the chamber

chapter 52 – one year there

    another cold winter day in january
    was my best day in korea
    when i was huddled
    in the back of a three-quarter ton
    in the early morning darkness
    being driven to kimpo airbase
    for processing out of korea
    after one year there

    i was processing out of korea
    eager to board a northwest orient jet
    and repeat the fourteen hour flight
    eager to board a big red tailed plane
    fulfilling the one dream
    of all soldiers
    to go home

    my final days i recorded
    on a short-timer's calendar
    typical of everyone in korea
    proudly taped to the door

of his locker

coloring each passing day

marking his last ninety days

until with clipboard in hand

the short-timer processes out

near the end

of my ninety days

there were stories told

about a master sergeant who

patrolled the kimpo airbase

walking the terminal

a wolf hungry for soldiers

who thought they would

leave korea not inspected

with unpolished shoes

unpolished belt buckles

wrinkled uniforms or crooked medals

this master sergeant joyfully

deleted any such soldier

from his scheduled flight

sending him back to his camp

to try for another flight out

and to be again reviewed
by that master sergeant
and get his blessing to leave

an icy chill ran through me
as the master sergeant approached me
carefully eye-balling my uniform
he smiled
an old crusty vulture smile
deeply enjoying his assignment
of yanking soldiers
whose uniforms showed disrespect
by not conforming to military standards
he visibly loved those standards

seconds seem like minutes
during such a review
but he shook my hand
wishing me good luck
i had passed his inspection
and when the wheels lifted
from the korean runway
all on board wildly cheered

one year can be short or long

or it can last an eternity

with the end too far away to see

we were heading home after being

one year there

chapter 53 – my bones

my bones white splintered dried
under both the korean sun and frost
were exposed and scattered
pushed by water and wind
dragged by small animals
who would gnaw on my bones
thankful for the calcium found

in life i was a sergeant
and a husband and father
married first to the military
and that military searched
downriver beyond the bridge
that bridge where i drowned
trying to find my body

they did not find my body

it mattered not to me
although three soldiers walked
so near and they might have

seen me if they were not

caught up in their laughter

over my being drunk that day

but now my bones are gone

what was left by creatures

has long since gone to dust

i have watched my body

quickly waste to be only bones

watching those bones get moved

a few here and some over there

until i vanished completely

together with camp colbern

was there no more

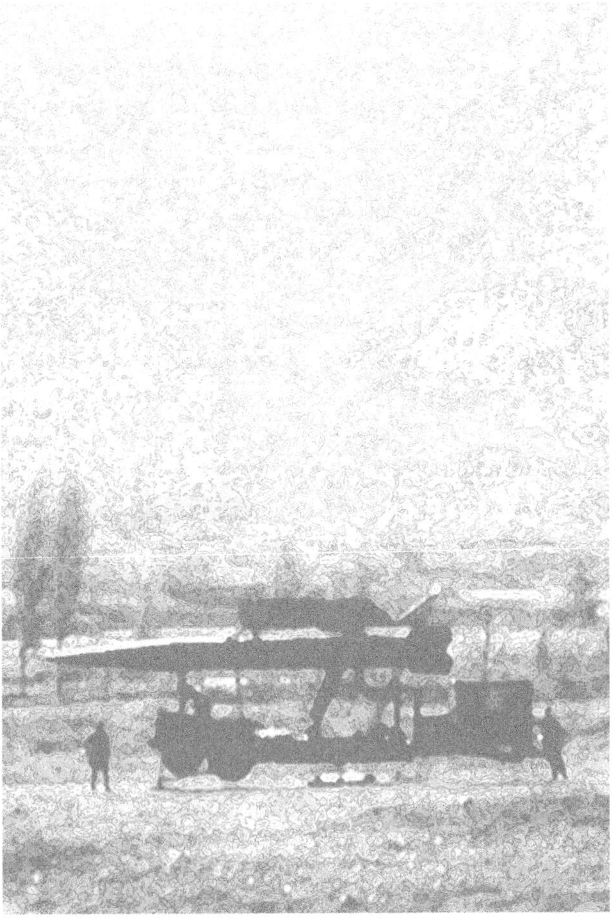

Made in United States
Orlando, FL
16 March 2024